T0273191

# PEYTON PLACE

David Trinidad

# Peyton Place

A Haiku Soap Opera

**TURTLE POINT PRESS**

NEW YORK

PUBLISHED BY TURTLE POINT PRESS

WWW.TURTLEPOINTPRESS.COM

COPYRIGHT © 2013 BY DAVID TRINIDAD

ALL RIGHTS RESERVED

ISBN 978-1-933527-81-9

LCCN 2012954366

PRINTED ON ACID-FREE, RECYCLED PAPER

IN THE UNITED STATES OF AMERICA

賢花 TRANSLATES AS SMART FLOWER,
DAVID TRINIDAD'S HAIKU PEN NAME

FOR BEC, CORA, AND JC

*my haiku support group*

## Cast

(IN ORDER OF APPEARANCE)

**DOROTHY MALONE** *Constance MacKenzie*

**RYAN O'NEAL** *Rodney Harrington*

**BARBARA PARKINS** *Betty Anderson*

**MIA FARROW** *Allison MacKenzie*

**CHRISTOPHER CONNELLY** *Norman Harrington*

**UNCREDITED** *Bud*

**KASEY ROGERS** *Julie Anderson*

**PAUL LANGTON** *Leslie Harrington*

**MARY ANDERSON** *Catherine Harrington*

**HENRY BECKMAN** *George Anderson*

**ED NELSON** *Dr. Michael Rossi*

**TIM O'CONNOR** *Elliot Carson*

**WARNER ANDERSON** *Matthew Swain*

**DAYNA CEDER** *Sharon Purcell*

SHERWOOD PRICE  *Roy Roberts*

ERIN O'BRIEN-MOORE  *Miss Choate*

KENT SMITH  *Dr. Robert Morton*

MICKY DOLENZ  *Kitch Brunner*

RICHARD EVANS  *Paul Hanley*

MARIETTE HARTLEY  *Claire Morton*

TED HARTLEY  *Rev. Jerry Bedford*

KIMBERLY BECK  *Kim Schuster*

EVELYN SCOTT  *Ada Jacks*

DON QUINE  *Joe Chernak*

PATRICIA MORROW  *Rita Jacks*

GAIL KOBE  *Doris Schuster*

WILLIAM SMITHERS  *David Schuster*

LESLIE NIELSEN  *Vincent Markham*

RICHARD DREYFUSS  *Student*

LESLIE NIELSEN  *Kenneth Markham*

LEE GRANT  *Stella Chernak*

JOHN KERR  *District Attorney John Fowler*

GREG MORRIS  *Officer Frank*

JOAN BLACKMAN *Marian Fowler*

DAVID CANARY *Russ Gehring*

LOLA ALBRIGHT *Constance Mackenzie*

GEORGE MACREADY *Martin Peyton*

JAMES DOUGLAS *Steven Cord*

BRUCE GORDON *Gus Chernak*

FRANK FERGUSON *Eli Carson*

DON GORDON *Richard Jensen*

SUSAN OLIVER *Ann Howard*

LANA WOOD *Sandy Webber*

STEPHEN OLIVER *Lee Webber*

RUTH WARRICK *Hannah Cord*

GARY HAYNES *Chris Webber*

DEREK SCHULTZ *Matthew Carson*

LEIGH TAYLOR-YOUNG *Rachel Welles*

JOHN KELLOGG *Jack Chandler*

GENA ROWLANDS *Adrienne Van Leyden*

DAN DURYEA *Eddie Jacks*

WILFRID HYDE-WHITE *Martin Peyton*

ROSE HOBART *Mary*

JOYCE JILLSON *Jill Smith*

MICHAEL CHRISTIAN *Joe Rossi*

ROBERT HOGAN *Rev. Tom Winter*

DIANA HYLAND *Susan Winter*

ELIZABETH "TIPPY" WALKER *Carolyn Russell*

BARBARA RUSH *Marsha Russell*

JOHN MARLEY *Rev. Gates*

PERCY RODRIGUES (AS PERCY RODRIGUEZ)
*Dr. Harry Miles*

RUBY DEE *Alma Miles*

GLYNN TURMAN *Lew Miles*

JOE MAROSS *Fred Russell*

FRANK LONDON *Charlie*

JOHN FINDLATER *Jeff Kramer*

JOAN VAN ARK (AS JOAN VAN ARC)
*Nurse Paula Dixon*

MARIO ALCALDE *Chuck Atwell*

JUDY PACE *Vickie Fletcher*

*This is the continuing story of Peyton Place . . .*

# Season One

EPISODES 1–114

1964–1965

**1**

Dolorous premiere.
Worth it for tidal wave of
Dorothy Malone's hair.

**2**

Ryan O'Neal fresh
from shower. Eyes glued to bare
chest, bulge in towel.

**3**

Betty has morning
sickness; Rod and Allison,
a date; Norm, wet pits.

## 4

Every episode
that same couple keeps crossing
the street, hand in hand.

## 5

Malone mugs with her
jaw, open mouth. O'Neal takes
off his tennis shirt.

## 6

Small-town slut Betty
ditches buff Bud to chase Rod,
the hunk who dumped her.

## 7

"Stars, I have seen them
fall . . ." Dreamy Mia Farrow
quotes A. E. Housman.

**8**

Who's she quoting now?
Something about leaves and snow.
No hits on Google.


**9**

Close-up of Barbara's
pained face. Pause DVD. Count
every single mole.


**1 0**

Contagious coiffure:
a surfer could shoot the curl
in Betty's mom's hair.


**1 1**

Betty finally tells
Rod she's preggers, but car crash
should take care of that.

## 1 2

Blonde nurse looks like she
was separated at birth
from Julia Stiles.


## 1 3

First she can't tell him
that she's knocked up, now she can't
tell him that she's not.


## 1 4

If you had to choose:
Connie's art or the owl lamp
at the Anderson's?


## 1 5

Despite his bad hair,
Norman's hot. Great playground shot:
his ass in white pants.

### 16

Can we talk about
Constance MacKenzie's big fat
black false eyelashes?

### 17

The only title
in paperback rack I can
make out is *The Robe*.

### 18

Watched this episode
twice and still can't come up with
idea for haiku.

### 19

At the hospital,
everyone's too worried to
notice the Grant Wood.

## 20

Odd frame: Norman bent
over water fountain. Is
he giving Dad head?

## 21

So much depended
upon sponsors: *Peyton Place*
*is brought to you by . . .*

## 22

Note the orderly.
No lines, but that look he gives
Malone speaks volumes.

## 23

Lies, secrets, gossip
and fucked-up families make this
black-and-white world tick.

## 2 4

Both brothers shirtless
in Norman's bedroom. Who cares
what's in Mother's will.


## 2 5

Did Dorothy dream I'd
gape, forty-five years later,
at her queer blonde hair?


## 2 6

For days I haven't
been able to get the theme
song out of my head.


## 2 7

After the credits,
autumn leaves litter the path.
Jealous George gets smashed.

### 2 8

Full moon, mist, Rossi
filmed through the neck of a lab
flask. Very arty.

### 2 9

Morality, truth,
courage, integrity—big
words for the small screen.

### 3 0

Will George see a shrink?
Carson be paroled? Connie
have a cavity?

### 3 1

Confessions and hard
facts, secret exits. Fake snow,
I have seen it fall.

*This is the continuing story of Peyton Place . . .*

EPISODES 32–65, RELEASED ON DVD JULY 14, 2009

## 3 2

Betty's still missing.
Carson comes home from prison.
Snow cloaks Peyton Place.

## 3 3

Phone call from Betty
cuts short the women's highly
caloric breakfast.

## 3 4

Julie and Connie
side by side—a virtual
tsunami of hair.

## 3 5

How much did it cost
Fox to stage a snowball fight
on SoCal back lot?

## 3 6

Malone's sweater's so
full, she almost pokes O'Neal
in front of fireplace.

## 3 7

Drama is promised
and delivered: Allison's
zipper gets unstuck.

## 3 8

I thought Connie's taste
in art sucked. Wait till you see
Sharon's bird painting.

**3 9**

Mother-daughter chat
completely upstaged by cool
sixties throw pillows.

**4 0**

Roy, Betty's near-date
rapist, fears the whole building
will hear her (dubbed) cries.

**4 1**

All this talk about
existentialist despair.
Then there's Norman's jeans.

**4 2**

Quite a basket on
guy who ogles Allison.
Big college welcome.

### 4 3

At the annual
faculty art exhibit,
more horrors await.

### 4 4

They just keep talking.
I guess every episode
is nothing but talk.

### 4 5

The cameraman
certainly has a yen for
Norman's tight trousers.

### 4 6

Last episode, Rod
gave Betty a nice hard slap.
Now it's back to talk.

**47**

Crotch watcher says: Rod
shows up for annulment not
wearing underwear.


**48**

We've seen some strange things,
but nothing as bizarre as
Betty's hand puppet.


**49**

Harrington brothers
in profile. Were they cast 'cause
they have the same nose?


**50**

What would a haiku
soap opera be without
an evil head nurse?

### 5 1

Am I wrong, or does
Dr. Morton don a dish
towel as a scarf?

### 5 2

Too perfect: Micky
Dolenz (future Monkee) slips
Norman a mickey.

### 5 3

Bullies tie up Norm
in town square, leave him to freeze.
Your standard hate crime.

### 5 4

Those ruffled kitchen
curtains: a Roy Lichtenstein
postcard I once sent.

## 5 5

The two hipsters who
strut through the hospital are
so on the wrong set.

## 5 6

We should all be paged
by a voice that comatose
at least once in life.

## 5 7

Didn't hear a word.
Too busy revising last
episode's haiku.

## 5 8

*Preview:* Shooting at
the Harrington house. I hope
it's not Elliot.

### 5 9

Ambulance siren
wails in the night. They milk it,
so why shouldn't I?

### 6 0

Ryan and Barbara
finally get star billing.
Elliot fights death.

### 6 1

I'm sorry, but they
mean to draw attention to
Norman's endowment.

### 6 2

Through the picket fence,
at the end of the brick walk,
lurks the Big Secret.

### 6 3

Is Allison's dream
world shattered by the truth or
by Hanley's bad art?

### 6 4

As Elliot's wheeled
out of surgery, the tide
(Connie's hair) is high.

### 6 5

Much has been revealed.
But not the release date of
the next installment.

*This is the continuing story of Peyton Place . . .*

*One year has passed. This*
*bootlegged "complete series" will*
*get me back on track.*

### 6 6

Mia can't forgive
Dorothy's deception. I still
can't forgive her hair.

### 6 7

More surprising than
her secret marriage is Claire
Morton's childhood doll.

## 6 8

In his hospital
room, Elliot clasps Connie's
unmoisturized hand.


## 6 9

The new priest prefers
Chopin, knows how to arrange
gladioli. Gay?


## 7 0

I wouldn't have missed
Connie's wedding *or* Norman's
outburst for the world.


## 7 1

When was the last time
you heard Proust referred to in
a soap opera?

### 7 2

"I'm still a growing
boy," Norman says, and his snug
corduroys prove it.


### 7 3

Connie mopes around
her Boston honeymoon suite.
Twin beds—I'd mope too.


### 7 4

For all the drama,
including a lost deaf girl,
really rather dull.


### 7 5

Allison's front-door
kiss is sweet. Still, keep your eyes
on her roving nose.

### 7 6

Dark night: Norman broods.
Rodney tries to counsel him,
basket center-frame.

### 7 7

I don't care about
these people's problems. All I
want is my haiku.

### 7 8

Allison trapped in
baby-sitting hell. Just smack
that bratty deaf girl!

### 7 9

Ada Jacks' costume
necklace—flashy. Connie's new
sweep of hair—flash flood.

## 80

Passing orderly
could be Ashbery. Did John
ever do walk-ons?

## 81

I've been misspelling
"MacKenzie." Per Constance's
shop window, small "k."

## 82

Miss Choate, that vicious
nagging witch of a nurse, won't
get off Betty's back.

## 83

This haiku goes out
to the lean extra and her
scene-stealing white pumps.

## 84

I can't help but trust
a doctor who thoroughly
enjoys a good smoke.


## 85

Why should Elliot
envy the handsome, deep-voiced,
tall, hunky salesman?


## 86

Really, this deaf girl
needs a walloping. She's spoiled
as Helen Keller.


## 87

Joe Chernak is our
new thug. But that's OK. He's
also our new stud.

## 88

Rita harassed by
Joe. Lightning illuminates
her white overbite.


## 89

It's already the
preview? What the hell happened
in this episode?


## 90

Everyone's slapping
and slugging each other. Then:
Boston bus cracks up.


## 91

Elliot gives blood
for crash victims. The Schusters
give each other slaps.

### 9 2

No hint of Leslie
Nielsen's comic genius in
this stiff performance.

### 9 3

Kim's no saint, but her
pigtail-pulling tormentors
should be tanned alive.

### 9 4

Handing out caps and
gowns: future Oscar winner
Richard Dreyfuss, ham.

### 9 5

After Joe molests
Rita, she runs home to dress.
Prom night is prom night.

## 96

Lower right corner:
Romance Classics' heart covers
Rita's tear-streaked face.

## 97

Prom music's getting
on Nielsen's nerves; his stilted
dialogue, on mine.

## 98

I'm not a breast man,
so Doris' nipples are
of little interest.

## 99

The second Leslie
Nielsen (city slicker twin)
is worse than the first.

### 100

At least the hundredth
episode rates a few new
exterior shots.


### 101

Cute bit: phone wakes Rod
at 5:00 a.m. and he tries
to answer his shoe.


### 102

Ada's got Connie
beat when it comes to thick, black
supersized lashes.


### 103

Lunch box Allison
gives Rod—if I can find it
on eBay, I'll bid.

## 104

First glimpse of Lee Grant,
fresh from being blacklisted,
in shiny black wig.

## 105

Hand on newspaper,
Norman clearly gives Rodney
his middle finger.

## 106

I swear one of the
old biddies on the park bench
is a man in drag.

## 107

Piroshki are small
Russian pastries filled with chopped
meat or vegetables.

### 108

How to fake clambake:
rear project ocean, wiggle
a rubber lobster.

### 109

With lines like these, it's
no wonder Nielsen's on his
way back to Peru.

### 110

Talk about buildup.
Is this Schuster bash ever
going to happen?

### 111

See if you can catch,
in the midst of Connie's kitsch,
van Gogh's masterpiece.

## 1 1 2

Great sound effects when
Rod and Joe fight are wasted
on deaf witness Kim.

## 1 1 3

Spoiler alert: Joe
drops dead. So will Doris'
party, if word spreads.

## 1 1 4

This is the way the
season ends, not with a bang
but a ringing phone.

*This is the continuing story of Peyton Place . . .*

# Season Two

EPISODES 115–267

**1965–1966**

## 115

Joe's death may have dashed
the party, but the cast at
last begins to act.

## 116

"You're a sucker for
punishment," Stella says to
Rossi. So am I.

## 117

John Kerr's hotness is
seriously undermined
by his goofy grin.

## 118

"Look," snaps Rod, "I signed
a statement. End of sonnet."
End of haiku, too.


## 119

Allison gets Kim
to talk. Trust me, so not *The
Miracle Worker*.


## 120

In the thick of it,
some doofus seeks a book on
Samuel Beckett.


## 121

Could Stella have worn
a frumpier hat to her
brother's funeral?

### 122

One of the combs in
that counter display would do
Norm a world of good.

### 123

Locked in his jail cell,
Rod's missing out on a lot
of tedious scenes.

### 124

Shades on, Malone makes
an entrance like the Oscar
winner that she is.

### 125

Artist on the wharf
staring at Stella, you're the
strangest extra yet.

### 126

The ratings must have
needed a boost: Allison's
run down by a car.

### 127

In fab, full-skirted
floral frock, Constance rushes
to the hospital.

### 128

Remember letters?
Bulldog Drummond? What about
cigarette machines?

### 129

Carmen Miranda
would laugh at the pathetic
fruit on that beach hat.

### 130

I see that Lee Grant's
scenery-chewing has earned
her "Guest Star" status.

### 131

Allison's poem.
No loss to literature
she's in a coma.

### 132

Nodding-off black cop
will soon rocket to *Mission:
Impossible* fame.

### 133

Can't take much more of
Allison's sophomoric
poetry *or* prose.

### 1 3 4

People, there's a huge
dent in Mrs. Fowler's car.
Hit-and-run. Hello!

### 1 3 5

This episode has
more than met the quota for
brunettes with secrets.

### 1 3 6

She wouldn't have hit
Allison if she'd had her
glare-free Foster Grants.

### 1 3 7

"Out, out, gravy spot . . ."
Dabbing Rod's black and red tie,
Norm sullies the Bard.

### 138

How many costumes
were cut from the same bolt of
polka-dotted cloth?

### 139

Long before there was
Court TV, there was Rodney
Harrington's hearing.

### 140

When Stella perjures
herself on the stand, Rod cries
"That's a lie!"—nine times.

### 141

Connie gets her test
results. Just what this messed-up
soap needs: more children.

### 142

I'm not sure lying
motionless in bed should be
considered acting.

### 143

Would you want Charles
Dickens read to you if you
were in a coma?

### 144

Betty alludes to
Orwell when her name is paged:
"Big Brother calling."

### 145

Allison's hand moved!
Looks like *Great Expectations*
is doing the trick.

### 146

Rossi sees movement
in her eye; direction, no.
Kinda like this show.

### 147

Snooping into Miss
Choate's files: Betty Anderson,
candy-striper sleuth.

### 148

Oh goody, Stella's
lies are beginning to catch
up with her. Squirm, bitch!

### 149

Turns out Miss Choate has
a heart, as well as an old
spaniel named Brandy.

### 1 5 0

The way Rodney strokes
his comatose girlfriend makes
me a bit nervous.

### 1 5 1

So many bad lines
and actors to poke fun at,
so few syllables.

### 1 5 2

For a D.A., you
sure are slow, Fowler. Russ has
the hots for your wife!

### 1 5 3

Allison wakes to
find her mother's been replaced
by Lola Albright.

## 154

Amnesia might be
a blessing—best to forget
she's part of this script.

## 155

Remind me never
to whiz to dinner in an
electric wheelchair.

## 156

Norm's wet underarms—
proof he's yet to discover
Arrid Extra Dry.

## 157

Grandfather Peyton
has furnished the mansion with
all sorts of Fox props.

## 158

Don't worry, Ryan,
in ten years you'll be the star
of a Kubrick film.

## 159

Attorney Steven
Cord both shadowboxes and
pussyfoots around.

## 160

Does everyone in
this town eat dinner at the
Colonial Inn?

## 161

HAIKU IN THE TRADITIONAL MANNER

The first day
of Rod's murder trial—
autumn wind

### 162

We've all got courtroom
nerves, I know, but these jerky
panning shots must stop.

### 163

If Norman were at
Disneyland, statue of Abe
Lincoln would talk back.

### 164

Impersonating
Martin Peyton, Bar-ba-rah
sound like Chinaman.

### 165

Let's see how many
lies Stella can tell with her
mouth full of eel sauce.

### 166

Betty takes the stand
(Do I smell a cliffhanger?)
at episode's end.

### 167

Queen of misshapen
perma-waves, Dorothy Malone
returns as Constance.

### 168

Betty trades insults
with Stella. (I prayed, but she
didn't grab her wig.)

### 169

Smoke all you want in
the courthouse, folks. Secondhand
risks don't exist yet.

## 170

Suppose the high point
of your acting career was
"courtroom spectator."

## 171

Can I skip this one?
Otherwise I'll have to write
about her stuffed toys.

## 172

I always cry when
dopes like Norman and Rita
secretly elope.

## 173

She calls him "husband."
He calls her "wife." I call *them*
insufferable.

## 174

Rita's middle name:
Charmaine. One more useless fact
to take to the grave.

## 175

A second threshold?
I've reached *my* threshold for this
newlywed nonsense.

## 176

You may remember
mobster-faced Bruce Gordon from
*The Untouchables*.

## 177

This is ABC,
not the Actors Studio.
Please, Lee, tone it down.

### 178

Rod should have skipped bail.
The lame way he dances is
a far greater crime.

### 179

Where all the dropouts,
hippies, and hit-run drivers
go: San Francisco.

### 180

I half expected
Peyton to whisper "Rosebud"
and drop his snow globe.

### 181

Congrats to the queen
who choreographed the brief
but chic fashion show.

### 182

Writers franticly
try to fit Mia's famous
haircut into script.

### 183

Shut up, Fowler! I
want to savour to the full
your wife's confession.

### 184

Somewhere in all these
theatrics, I know there's at
least one good haiku.

### 185

Guess that sums it up:
at a certain age it's ice
cream instead of sex.

### 186

My eyes popped out when
Rossi lit his cig next to
those oxygen tanks.


### 187

Rodney takes the stand
(Do I smell a cliffhanger?)
at episode's end.


### 188

She filled a scooped orange
with marshmallows and sardines?
Divorce Rita, Norm.


### 189

Just admit it: you
enjoyed Steven's badgering
of deaf witness Kim.

### 190

Closing arguments
were a snorefest—beyond the
shadow of a doubt.

### 191

Short-haired Mia rocks
antique cradle—presage of
*Rosemary's Baby*.

### 192

The verdict is in.
Pity it breaks up brothers'
softcore wrestling match.

### 193

Rodney found guilty!
I haven't felt this outraged
since the O.J. trial.

### 194

Enter the thug from
Stella's past. *Preview:* he grips
her wig with both fists!

### 195

As my therapist
would tell you, Stella, actions
have consequences.

### 196

I'd think twice about
tossing around phrases like
"phony dramatics."

### 197

They love Allison's
bad writing. She'd do well in
the poetry world.

### 198

Caught with a purse full
of pinched dope, Stella admits
she lied under oath.

### 199

Explain to me why
Fowler ties his shoe in the
middle of this scene.

### 200

Rossi saves Constance
from washing her hair. Who'll save
us until she does?

### 201

Either someone off
screen's munching Lay's, or that fake
snow's mighty crunchy.

### 202

Schuster resigns from
the Peyton Mill. Just like that,
written off the show.

### 203

Suddenly it's spring.
The day Betty weds Steven.
But does she love him?

### 204

Here comes the bride, all
dressed in white, with an extra
as maid of honor.

### 205

Honestly, Malone
has two hairstyles in one scene.
Continuity!

### 206

Plot tease: why has this
mysterious blonde woman
come to Peyton Place?

### 207

Gonna need Julie's
mint-flavored tranquilizers
to keep writing these.

### 208

Distracted by Ann's
velvet bow hair clip. Who did
she push off the cliff?

### 209

Sandy (Lana Wood,
Natalie's sis) tries to hit
on Rod. Total slut!

## 2 1 0

Lee's got a greasy
job, wild wife, blind kid brother,
and bod to die for.

## 2 1 1

Playing blind man's bluff
on the bluff, a boy ended
up blind? Urban myth.

## 2 1 2

Rita doesn't want
to be pregnant. I don't want
her to be, either.

## 2 1 3

Speaking of pregnant,
Connie has a craving for
a banana split.

### 214

Since sarcasm is
Norm's natural state, he should
try writing haiku.


### 215

Watch when Dorothy bites
into her sandwich: lunchmeat
gets caught in her teeth.


BONUS TEXT MESSAGE

Hannah just revealed
that Ann Howard is Steven's
sister. OMG!


### 216

Doctors Hospital
would fall apart without the
efficient Miss Choate.

## 217

Slow buildup to Lee's
face-off with Ann leads to fast
zoom-in on his face.

## 218

Theme music: the bell
of transience. This boring
bluff subplot shall pass.

## 219

Allison was much
more interesting when she
was in a coma.

## 220

"A shabby little
grease spot on a dead-end street."
Best line in eons.

### 2 2 1

Climbing to the edge
of the bluff, Ann's feet sink in
the foam rubber rock.

### 2 2 2

Countless sixties chicks
mimicked Rita's perky flip
for their yearbook pics.

### 2 2 3

I was as stricken
as Ann when the blind guy tapped
his cane toward her.

### 2 2 4

Connie, Stella, Ann—
seems Rossi has a thing for
angst-ridden women.

### 225

Luckily, Lee's black
turtleneck and jeans couldn't
be any tighter.

### 226

It appears a rock
cod was harmed in the making
of this episode.

### 227

Sandy and Betty's
frenzied boob-jiggling dance off—
strange female custom.

### 228

Stuffed-shirt Steven calls
it "exhibitionism."
Six whole syllables!

### 229

They've doctored Catherine's
portrait to resemble Ann.
Get it? She's Ann's mom.


### 230

Lee threatens Ann in
parking lot. Betty finds slashed
painting in basement.


### 231

It's been worth thousands
of syllables just to hear
Rossi say one: "punk."


### 232

Allison can't hold
a guy like Rod with poems—
not the kind she writes.

### 233

The glycerin tear
running down Ann's face shines like
a slimy snail trail.

### 234

From behind, it looks
as if the blind guy has been
given a wedgie.

### 235

For Chrissakes, Betty,
Steven and Ann deserve to
know the truth. *Tell them.*

### 236

As the hearse passes,
Connie feels her baby kick.
Voilà, life and death.

### 237

Like many mothers,
Hannah's a whiz at lies and
manipulation.

### 238

Chris falls—again. Ann
takes the blame—again. While I
roll my eyes—again.

### 239

Unless she chills out,
Ann's obsession with Chris will
be her undoing.

### 240

Too-brief shot of Rod's
bubble butt. Could you move the
camera to the left?

### 2 4 1

Although Chris is blind,
he sees the bullshit behind
Lee's accusations.

### 2 4 2

Is a paperweight
the best gift to give a girl
who just lost her job?

### 2 4 3

Bored poet freezes
each frame of garage fistfight
to detect stunt men.

### 2 4 4

Sandy's "a real drag."
Lee wants "kicks." Soap opera hacks
knock off hip bar talk.

## 245

Seeing Betty in
such pain puts me in touch with
my inner sadist.


## 246

### JULY 19, 1966

On this day, Mia
married Frank Sinatra, three
decades her senior.


## 247

I guessed Lee did it
way back, but I'll act surprised
for your benefit.


## 248

Lee tries to blackmail
Les into hiring him. Tip
for the unemployed?

### 249

Chris calls Steven's bluff.
Bluff! Is that the only word
these characters know?

### 250

No time for retakes:
Chris flinched *before* Lee threw the
money in his face.

### 251

The facade of the
Webber's house is Ada Jacks'
house, merely with plants.

### 252

If you find yourself
rewinding to eye the blind
guy's bulge, step away.

### 253

Overwrought, Hannah
gets it on with the bust of
Marie Antoinette.


### 254

Can't believe they bumped
off Ann. Oh well. Live by the
bluff, die by the bluff.


### 255

This guy's forever
walking in front of cars. Buy
a Seeing Eye dog!


### 256

Susan Oliver—
best known as green-skinned Vina
in *Star Trek* pilot.

### 257

Hypocrisy, lies
and deceit—Rod may not like
it, but we sure do.


### 258

Why am I entranced
with the pitiful contents
of a dead girl's purse?


### 259

Lee doth protest too
much, methinks, when policeman
firmly pats him down.


### 260

Ceaseless table talk
keeps Steven from taking one
bite of Betty's roast.

### 261

Did Hannah kill Ann?
Is Allison cracking up?
Rod packing a sock?

### 262

I beg to differ:
out-of-shape Rossi *does* need
a fitness lecture.

### 263

Troubled Allison
disappears so Mia can
pursue film career.

### 264

Miss Choate chokes up; she
knows ratings will plummet with
no Mia Farrow.

## 265

You boys won't find her.
She's not in the opening
credits anymore.


## 266

Connie's expected
to give birth in ten days—to
a lumpy pillow.


## 267

At its height, show aired
thrice weekly. That's why Season
Two is so damn long.


*This is the continuing story of Peyton Place . . .*

# Season Three

EPISODES 268–368

**1966–1967**

### 268

The first episode
"In Color." I feel like I
just landed in Oz.

### 269

Connie goes into
labor in her blue bathrobe,
next to the orange lamp.

### 270

It's a boy! Meanwhile,
Peyton plots to stop Steven
from defending Lee.

### 271

Hannah's henna rinse
matches the décor on two
consecutive sets.

### 272

For court, Steven makes
Lee change his flashy tie. But
not his holey sock?

### 273

Rossi testifies.
Ann's death already distant,
a black-and-white dream.

### 274

Few things are dumber
than Norm's imitation of
W. C. Fields.

## 275

John Kerr's baby blues—
too bad they grace the same face
as that goofball grin.

## 276

Lee, shirtless, doing
jail cell push-ups. The utmost
of hunkalicious.

## 277

While camping, Norman
and Rita find wild girl in
abandoned cabin.

## 278

Who is this strange young
woman, and how did she get
Allison's bracelet?

### 279

Connie, there is no
need to put those plastic red
roses in water.

### 280

Van Gogh's masterpiece
now hangs in Rossi's office.
Musical Fox prop.

### 281

Rodney confuses
his grandfather's afternoon
nap for the big sleep.

### 282

Norman likes Rita
to wear her hair short so she'll
look like a boy. Huh.

## 283

Sucky new subplot
(abused orphan) makes me miss
all that bluff business.

## 284

Whose bright idea was
it to place a dish rack in
front of Rachel's face?

## 285

Rod and Norman drink
radioactive orange pop.
Crank call spooks Connie.

## 286

Ada Jacks is more
colorful "In Color" than
the whole cast combined.

## 287

Drunk, Steven cries "I'm
a human being" à la
the Elephant Man.

## 288

On the stand, Peyton
fakes chest pains just as Steven
cross-examines him.

## 289

Beware of sleazeball
child-abusing uncles who
barge in bearing sweets.

## 290

Boring episode
includes scripture about truth
(John 8:32).

### 291

Boring episode
includes home remedy for
scars: cocoa butter.

### 292

The so-called traffic—
just a couple cars that keep
driving round the square.

### 293

How many of us
would love to get our mother
on the witness stand?

### 294

Never grill your own
mother unless you're sure she's
really your mother.

## 295

Visiting Catherine's
grave, white-haired Martin Peyton
leans on his two canes.

## 296

The redone portrait
of Catherine Harrington looms—
a bit cross-eyed, no?

## 297

Let's hope there are more
opportunities to see
Steven's hairy chest.

## 298

Chris wears red sweater
vest; Sandy, lavender coat.
Oh, and Lee goes free.

### 299

We'll let you keep your
gay card if you swoon over
Rachel's chiffon dress.


### 300

Norman pretty much
breaks the fourth wall when he says
no one's listening.


### 301

If Hannah hadn't
set fire to Catherine's portrait,
I would have bupkis.


### 302

Steven saves Martin
from the burning mansion. Will
the old coot pull through?

### 303

In real life, Lana
Wood and Steve Oliver were
married—for one month.

### 304

Loathsome Lee Webber
finally meets his match in
no-nonsense Miss Choate.

### 305

Oh please, what is Chris
(who's blind, remember) going
to do with a gun?

### 306

Lee's jeans are so tight
you'd think he's the one with the
pistol in his pants.

### 307

Insanity is
rewatching this episode
expecting haiku.

### 308

Now Norman's doing
a dumb imitation of
Little Caesar, see.

### 309

Chris plans to kill Lee.
Jack stalks Rachel. Tension builds
counting syllables.

### 310

It was easier
to torment baby-sitters
pre-caller ID.

### 3 1 1

Chris will miss. (Don't you
hate when the preview gives the
cliffhanger away?)


### 3 1 2

Elliot objects
to his son's lace christening gown.
Homophobic much?


### 3 1 3

Ryan looks up to
remind the lazy stagehands
to sprinkle fake snow.


### 3 1 4

Dizziness in the
kitchen. Does Rita have a
bun in the oven?

### 315

Nope, it's worse than that:
Rita might have symptoms of
mitral stenosis.


### 316

FEBRUARY 27, 1967

Ironically, Leigh
and Ryan marry the day
they break up on show.


### 317

Ever dense, Rita
misses the significance
of Rachel's secret.


### 318

In gray hat and coat,
Les gives Rod the third degree
like a noir flatfoot.

### 319

Got so involved in
the stupid plot, forgot to
look for things to mock.

### 320

Rachel, sleuthing in
basement, is startled by Jack.
This is getting good!

### 321

Guess who clobbers Jack
with the candlestick in the
farmhouse. Miss Scarlett?

### 322

Tearjerker alert:
Carsons welcome Rachel home.
Have Kleenex handy.

### 3 2 3

But not when Norman
breaks down—unless bad acting
makes you laugh to tears.

### 3 2 4

To the already
long list of Lee's faults can be
added litterbug.

### 3 2 5

Peyton's money turns
Steven on. That blue Princess
phone does it for me.

### 3 2 6

Lee assaults Rachel.
Maybe the dumb bunny should
stay out of basements.

### 327

Has Martin written
Rod and Norm out of the will?
Or better yet, script?

### 328

From soap to sitcom:
Betty's mom switched to *Bewitched*
(second Louise Tate).

### 329

Immorality.
I love how that fills the line.
Im-mo-ral-i-ty.

### 330

Les blackmails Betty
to break into Martin's safe.
Hitchcock-like suspense.

### 331

Betty, I'll give you
seventeen syllables to
spill contents of will.

### 332

"The Waste Land"? One of
the writers is showing off
their English degree.

### 333

Haven't seen Miss Choate
in a while. Oops, spoke too soon . . .
camera passed her by.

### 334

So how will tying
Rita to bed keep her from
getting excited?

### 3 3 5

Carson beats up Jack,
is jailed. I can't do any
more time in that cell.


### 3 3 6

Even Jack Chandler,
nefarious as he is,
fears sharp-tongued nurse Choate.


### 3 3 7

His fifteen seconds:
Ray, beer-drinking extra with
one line: "Thanks, Ada."


### 3 3 8

It only hurts Jack
when he laughs. Ha! It only
hurts me when I watch.

### 339

The van Gogh lands back
in Connie's shop. A prop is
a prop is a prop.

### 340

Jack hightails it out
of town. You say criminal,
I say sensible.

### 341

His name, Mr. Teal,
just so happens to be the
color of his phone.

### 342

Betty's "party girl"
past (see episode 40)
comes back to haunt her.

**3 4 3**

Kids, dogs, and clutter.
Rita's dream of happiness
would be my nightmare.

**3 4 4**

Dorothy's wig—one huge
blonde wave that, as it crashes,
is hair-sprayed in place.

**3 4 5**

Did any fans dial
555-3626
and ask for Steven?

**3 4 6**

Lana Wood's swan song.
Slow zoom on her face, worried
about her next job.

**3 4 7**

Aunt Lucy's Bible
is full of secrets—none of
which will save your soul.


**3 4 8**

Just when you think you
can trust someone, they turn out
to be the Bad Seed.


**3 4 9**

I do not know which
to prefer: Shakespeare quote or
pillow fight after.


**3 5 0**

Stuffed bird and weirdo
behind desk—is Jack checking
into Bates Motel?

### 3 5 1

Rachel kidnaps the
baby, yes, but in preview
Betty and Rod kiss.


### 3 5 2

Something I learned long
ago, Connie: never turn
down a sedative.


### 3 5 3

Two policemen shoot
at and chase Chandler. All three
of them run like girls.


### 3 5 4

Leigh will one day win
Emmy, but not for losing
her mind on this show.

### 355

Here's Gena Rowlands,
Mrs. John Cassavetes,
much-needed fresh blood.

### 356

Relax, Rita won't
croak. Her weak heart will tick till
this soap gets canceled.

### 357

Jack escapes from jail
and takes off to do guest spots
on TV Westerns.

### 358

Whack! Nothing ends an
episode better than a
good slap in the face.

### 359

And nothing starts an
episode better than a
repeat of that slap.

### 360

"Again" (Fox standard)
is always playing at the
Colonial Inn.

### 361

Step right up, folks, and
witness Rod's imitation
of a barking seal.

### 362

This is just to say
Elliot ate an apple—
Golden Delicious.

### 363

Eddie Jacks, deadbeat
husband and dad—back to cause
all kinds of havoc.

### 364

Martin's clearly not
his right self: he's been replaced
by Wilfrid Hyde-White.

### 365

In what musical
did Hyde-White play Pickering?
I think you've got it.

### 366

Adulterous kiss
on the beach. New England sure
looks like Malibu.

### 3 6 7

The mystery of
Betty's portrait—different
each time we see it.

### 3 6 8

This isn't the first
season that's ended with a
ringing telephone.

*In Color, the continuing story of Peyton Place . . .*

# Season Four

EPISODES 369–460

**1967–1968**

**3 6 9**

Would it have killed them
to put some pizazz in the
season opener?

**3 7 0**

Betty and Steven's
marriage is in big trouble—
big as Gena's hair.

**3 7 1**

A smart haiku scribe
can avoid rewatching this
talky offering.

### 372

First scene proves there are
pervs who find Victorian
bric-a-brac sexy.

### 373

Bet you're dying to
hear Elliot tell the Greek
myth of Callisto.

### 374

Sorry, Betty. Your
tribulations get trumped by
Rod's tight-fitting tee.

### 375

HAIKU IN THE MODERN MANNER

The faces of these barflies in Ada's tavern;
Extras on a cheesy set.

### 376

Betty can't divorce
Steven fast enough now that
Rod's sniffin' around.

### 377

Well again, the real
Martin resumes his "grotesque
manipulations."

### 378

Rossi's medical
jargon sounds like pig Latin
to me too, Eddie.

### 379

If you must speak ill
of the dead, Ada, please use
fewer syllables.

### 380

Betty admires the
changing leaves. What does she think
this is, a haiku?

### 381

Duryea, Sleaze King
of Noir, taunts Rowlands, Queen of
Independent Film.

### 382

Don't waste precious time.
Skip right to Rod and Betty's
climactic lip-lock.

### 383

Martin's sanity
hearing. So few sets, I knew
we'd be back in court.

### 384

Rita wants a boy.
(Have I mentioned she's with child?)
Les wants Peyton dead.

### 385

Betty sobs because
she and Steven are splitsville.
Say that ten times fast.

### 386

Chauvinism or
foreplay? Rod bids "wench" Betty
to take off his boots.

### 387

Do we really need
to know that Mary, Peyton's
maid, has bursitis?

### 388

The autumn leaves are
blowing, but only in front
of the camera.

### 389

A biker almost
runs over old man Peyton.
Otherwise, just talk.

### 390

Is it pointless to
scold a killer for his bad
telephone manners?

### 391

Today let's simply
enjoy the way these people
torment each other.

### 392

I did not expect
Gena to tumble to her
death. But now you will.

### 393

Betty flees in the
first snowfall of the season—
Season Four, that is.

### 394

Rita's collapsed. So
few sets, I knew we'd be back
in the hospital.

### 395

And of course we can't
let the jail cell sit empty.
Arrest Eddie Jacks.

### 396

I wish I had a
dime for every time Betty
has withheld the truth.

### 397

Takes a funeral
to make the remaining cast
act like they're alive.

### 398

Grant me an extra
syllable and I'll reveal
who Martin wants killed.

### 399

Grant me another
and I'll tell you who Martin
*really* wants done in.

### 400

Can't say I'll miss Lee.
He was a great hoodlum but
a lousy chauffeur.

### 401

Steve Oliver will
later star in the truly
bad *Werewolves on Wheels*.

### 402

Woman abandons
baby on wharf. Geez, give us
a second to breathe.

### 403

No wonder Jill runs
away when Connie calls her
Allison—that hair!

### 4 0 4

Lana Wood returns
to the show—thankfully just
for Lee's funeral.

### 4 0 5

Whatever Jill knows
about Allison, it's clear
that the writers don't.

### 4 0 6

You'll want nurse Choate to
be nearby the next time you
hyperventilate.

### 4 0 7

Heart surgery? We're
not leaving the hospital
set anytime soon.

### 408

Just watch me fit "closed
mitral valvulotomy"
into a haiku.

### 409

Maybe if Norm thinks
of a dead pet, he will cry
more convincingly.

### 410

Rita loses her
baby. Ryan loses his
lines discussing it.

### 411

Into town comes Joe,
Dr. Rossi's hot younger
bro. Well, semi-hot.

### 412

If Jill's baby, as
she says, is Allison's, is
Rod the father? *Zzzzz*.


### 413

Birth certificate
shows it's Rosemary's I mean
Allison's baby.


### 414

This 20-inch screen
isn't big enough for two
bleached blonde actresses.


### 415

Haiku or not, I'm
only going to watch this
episode one time.

## 416

Dorothy's enormous
bouffant flip might have earned her
a part in *Hairspray*.

## 417

Unless you *act* like
they're heavy, Joe, we'll know those
boxes are empty.

## 418

Joe and Norm involved
in car accident. Back to
hospital set, stat.

## 419

A new regular,
Tom Winter, pulls Norm and Joe
from overturned car.

### 420

Elliot speak like
Injun chief. He make PC
police heap-um mad.


### 421

Am I the only
one who wishes Rita had
died in surgery?


### 422

Meet Rev. Winter's
wife Susan, alky, blonde hair
teased to the rafters.


### 423

Jill's overwhelmed with
indifference. You see where
I'm going with this?

### 424

Can the minister
help Rita's marriage when his
own is such a mess?

### 425

Speaking of hopeless
couples, Betty's making plans
to remarry Rod.

### 426

Wake me when Norman's
done dialing Ada on
his rotary phone.

### 427

Rita relives her
trauma on the wharf. Ugh. That
means we have to too.

### 428

In the history
of her bad hair days, this is
Dorothy's Waterloo.

### 429

Taking a powder,
Eddie waves to no one as
the bus pulls away.

### 430

Connie's forced to give
up the baby, which is, duh,
Jill's, not Allison's.

### 431

Don't know about you,
but I'd rather not watch the
minister undress.

### 4 3 2

Exit Dan, enter
Tippy. In soaps the actors
come and go, talking.

### 4 3 3

Fun Fact: Barbara Rush
won a Golden Globe for *It
Came from Outer Space*.

### 4 3 4

The reverend and his
wife have shouting match in house
of God. Does He hear?

### 4 3 5

Malone's quit the show!
oh Dorothy Malone we love
your bad hair come back

## 436

Betty Anderson
Harrington Cord Harrington.
Shades of Liz Taylor!


## 437

Carsons gone. Mill sold.
Heraclitus says, "All is
flux, nothing stays still."


## 438

Okay, okay, Joe's
got a hot little body.
Are you happy now?


## 439

So it's come to this—
syllable-counting fingers
waking me from sleep.

**440**

"Grooving with a guy"—
1968 code for
"fucking your brains out."


**441**

Yes, Susan, spell it
out. After that last haiku,
nothing will shock us.


**442**

It only takes one
bad apple to spoil the whole
Love Generation.


**443**

Tom pops a telltale
boner when he gives Jill a
ministerly hug.

**444**

When you drunkenly
fall out of bed, your day can
only get better.

**445**

They took their sweet time
removing Malone from the
opening credits.

**446**

If praying doesn't
work, Tom, may I suggest you
take a cold shower?

**447**

What fun's being wed
to a reverend if you can't
cause his fall from grace?

### 448

I, too, dislike it:
there are more important things
than Marsha's love life.

### 449

Such as crashing a
motorcycle. That should help
keep our minds off sex.

### 450

Won't know how Rod is
till after surgery. Thank
God nurse Choate's on shift.

### 451

Succumbing to the
evils of the flesh, Tom lays
a wet one on Jill.

### 452

Rod may never walk
again. My poor fingers may
never stop counting.

### 453

Still getting used to
seeing third-rate Ed Nelson
in Malone's star spot.

### 454

Tom, nobody, not
even a man of God, can
boss Miss Choate around.

### 455

Some feeling returns
to Rod's left hand. You see where
I'm going with this?

### 456

Now that he's lost his
faith, I'm more than happy to
watch Tom lose his shirt.

### 457

You'll want nurse Choate to
be nearby the next time you're
on a drunken tear.

### 458

Everyone knows John
Marley from *The Godfather*'s
horse-head-in-bed scene.

### 459

Middle-aged couples
seriously sucking face
in public: Yes/No?

**460**

Though ratings are poor,
the story of Peyton Place
keeps continuing.

# Season Five

EPISODES 461–514

**1968–1969**

Rod's still paralyzed
from the waist down. Don't look at
me. I'm not *that* crass.

Is Betty boffing
ex-husband Steven now that
Rod can't get ~~it~~ up?

The passing seasons
have bestowed on the owl lamp
a tackier shade.

## 464

Betty and Rod speak
of the woe that is in their
soap opera marriage.

## 465

Susan and Tom speak
of the woe that is in *their*
soap opera marriage.

## 466

Not that I'm counting,
but I've got forty-eight more
episodes to go.

## 467

When the first black guest
star says "we've come a long way,"
he isn't kidding.

## 468

Rossi, must you waste
what few syllables we have
indulging a lush?

## 469

Harry, Alma, Lew,
Fred, Charlie, Jeff, Carolyn.
Who *are* these people?

## 470

*I* know what "mental
cruelty" means: four hundred
seventy haiku.

## 471

If you can ever
see Michael Christian in *Poor
Pretty Eddie*, don't.

## 472

DVD froze just
as Joe and Jill finally
admitted they love

## 473

Joe and Jill tie knot,
leave town. No place in Peyton
for happy couples.

## 474

'Tis better to be
paged than seen: "Miss Choate, pick up
on line 22."

## 475

*Knots Landing* diva
Joan Van Ark made her humble
start here, as a nurse.

### 476

Martin Peyton is
dead. Now the old bastard can
manipulate God.


### 477

Three episodes and
Miss Choate still hasn't picked up
on line 22.


### 478

Marsha's obsessed with
her daughter's maidhood. Aren't there
support groups for that?


### 479

You, who hold this in
your hand, do you know what a
mimeograph was?

### 480

Dadaist Susan
suggests putting a mustache
on Betty's portrait.


### 481

Beauty is not truth
when Betty is involved. That's
all ya need to know.


### 482

Chaucer, yes, but why
must we drag poor Keats through the
pop culture gutter?


### 483

Best thing I can say
about this episode is
it put me to sleep.

### 484

Let Betty and Chuck
ramble on. I'm under the
spell of the owl lamp.

### 485

Rod's homecoming. I
can nail this haiku as he
hobbles to the door.

### 486

Guess who's coming to
dinner at the black family's
house. Nervous white folks.

### 487

Poor Eli, playing
checkers all by himself. Don't
ever be eighty.

### 488

"I'm Fred, an aging
Lothario, home-breaker,
and fool. Who are you?"

### 489

Barbara Rush was once
married to fifties "beefcake
boy" Jeffrey Hunter.

### 490

Eli quotes *A Tale
of Two Cities*. Just "the worst
of times" applies here.

### 491

There's no way you can
convince me they're not playing
Rod's relapse for laughs.

## 492

Harry tries to bribe
Vickie, who's blackmailing Lew.
Twenty-two to go.

## 493

It should come as no
surprise that Rod's problem is
Betty, not his spine.

## 494

Norman's diatribe
disrupts the effect of Rod's
sleeping pill. Killjoy.

## 495

An antique Bible
box. Gee, thanks, Mike. It's just what
I've always wanted.

### 496

Rod will wish he had
Peyton's fortune when he gets
his hospital bills.

### 497

AFTER JOE BRAINARD

I hope you have enjoyed not reading this haiku as
much as I have enjoyed not writing it.

### 498

Carolyn calls Fred
a bigot—but says nothing
about Marsha's brooch!

### 499

No matter how much
Barbara overacts, she can't
distract from that brooch.

## 500

Even though the show's
in color, the town's uptight
about black and white.

## 501

Farewell, Ryan. *Love
Story*, Farrah, and bloated
old age await you.

## 502

Percy Rodrigues
*has* come a long way—to the
opening credits.

## 503

Don't you hate it when
you tell someone you love them
and they say "I know"?

### 504

Took five long seasons
for Mike to find the right girl
(with a psycho ex).

### 505

AFTER BUSON

Boring episode—
yet it will be remembered
thanks to this haiku.

### 506

Lew's phonograph and
typewriter—I weep like a
luddite for the past.

### 507

Unflappable Miss
Choate, clothed in pink, I think I'll
miss you most of all.

### 508

The great Ruby Dee
is still going strong. Let's hear
it for Ruby Dee!

### 509

At this point, Fred's death
won't make much difference to
anyone but him.

### 510

After he's booked, Mike
uses TP to wipe ink
off his fingertips.

### 511

Marsha and Mike make
out in jail cell—not quite as
sexy as it sounds.

## 512

Do not go gentle,
soap fans. Rage, rage against the
show's cancellation.

## 513

AFTER SHIKI

Write me down as one
who loved poetry and the
paste jewels of pop art.

## 514

Marsha couldn't have
been less credible if she'd
worn her brooch in court.

**THE END**

# Murder in Peyton Place

MADE-FOR-TV MOVIE

**1977**

Once you see how much
the actors have aged, you won't
care who gets murdered.

# Peyton Place:
# The Next Generation

MADE-FOR-TV MOVIE

**1985**

They may be young and
cute, but they're doomed to repeat
the same storylines.

Portions of this work previously appeared in
*The Best American Poetry 2013* (Scribner, 2013),
*The Broome Street Review*, *Carbon Copy
Magazine*, *Columbia Poetry Review*, *Lo-Ball*,
*PANK*, *Poem-A-Day* (Poets.org/The Academy
of American Poets), *Painted Bride Quarterly,
Puerto del Sol*, *Rabbit Ears: TV Poems*
(Poets Wear Prada, 2013), and *Stolen Island*.

The first sixty-five haiku were published
in *Dear Prudence: New and Selected Poems*
(Turtle Point Press, 2011).

## David Trinidad's

*Dear Prudence: New and Selected Poems*
was published in 2011 by Turtle Point
Press. He is also the editor of *A Fast Life:
The Collected Poems of Tim Dlugos*
(Nightboat Books, 2011). Trinidad lives
in Chicago, where he teaches poetry
at Columbia College and co-edits
the journal *Court Green*.